Bananas on My Table

Eduardo Aparicio

Rigby®
A Harcourt Achieve Imprint

www.Rigby.com
1-800-531-5015

The bananas are
on the tree.

The bananas are
on the boat.

5

The bananas are
on the ship.

The bananas are
on the train.

The bananas are
on the truck.

The bananas are
in the store.

13

The bananas are
in the cart.

15

The bananas are on my table!